SEQUOIA
NATIONAL PARK
ACTIVITY BOOK

PUZZLES, MAZES, GAMES, AND MORE ABOUT
SEQUOIA NATIONAL PARK

NATIONAL PARKS ACTIVITIES SERIES

SEQUOIA NATIONAL PARK ACTIVITY BOOK

Copyright 2021
Published by Little Bison Press

The author acknowledges that the land that is now Sequoia National Park are the traditional lands of the Western Mono (Monache), the Foothills Yokuts, and the Tubatulabal People.

LITTLE BISON
Press

For more free national parks activities, visit
Littlebisonpress.com

About Sequoia National Park

Sequoia National Park is located in the state of California. People from all over the world come to visit Sequoia National Park to see the namesake giant sequoias, some of the biggest trees in the world. Sequoia National Park is located adjacent to Kings Canyon National Park. It was established as a national park in 1890.

Sequoia National Park is home to Tharp's Log, a cabin formed out of a hollowed-out giant sequoia log. Hale Tharp was one of the first non-Native people to visit the area. Tharp established a small summer cattle ranch at Giant Forest. He made a cabin out of a fallen log. The log was hollowed by fire through fifty-five feet of its seventy-foot length. If you hike the Crescent Meadow Trail, you can visit the cabin and see the fireplace, door, and window at one end.

Sequoia National Park is famous for:
- Mt. Whitney, the tallest mountain in the lower 48 states
- Crescent Meadow, a sequoia ringed meadow in the Giant Forest
- groves of the big trees

Hey! I'm Parker!

I'm the only snail in history to visit every National Park in the United States! Come join me on my adventures in Sequoia National Park.

Throughout this book, we will learn about the history of the park, the animals and plants that live here, and things to do here if you ever get to visit in person. This book is also full of games and activities!

Last but not least, I am hidden 9 times on different pages. See how many times you can find me. This page doesn't count!

Sequoia National Park Bingo

Let's play bingo! Cross off each box that you are able to during your visit to the national park. Try to get a bingo down, across, or diagonally. If you can't visit the park, use the bingo board to plan your perfect trip.

Pick out some activities that you would want to do during your visit. What would you do first? How long would you spend there? What animals would you try to see?

SPOT A MAMMAL SMALLER THAN YOU	HUG A GIANT SEQUOIA	IDENTIFY A TREE	TAKE A PICTURE AT AN OVERLOOK	WATCH A MOVIE AT THE VISITORS CENTER
GO FOR A HIKE	LEARN ABOUT THE INDIGENOUS PEOPLE THAT LIVE IN THIS AREA	WITNESS A SUNRISE OR SUNSET	OBSERVE THE NIGHT SKIES	VISIT CRYSTAL CAVE
HEAR A BIRD CALL	SPOT A RUSHING RIVER	FREE SPACE	LEARN ABOUT THE IMPORTANCE OF FIRES	VISIT A RANGER STATION
PICK UP 10 PIECES OF TRASH	GO CAMPING	SEE A MULE DEER	VISIT THE GIANT FOREST	SPOT A BIRD OF PREY
LEARN ABOUT THE GEOLOGY OF THE SIERRAS	SEE SOMEONE RIDING A HORSE	HAVE A PICNIC	SPOT SOME ANIMAL TRACKS	PARTICIPATE IN A RANGER-LED ACTIVITY

The National Park Logo

The National Park System has over 400 units in the US. Just like Sequoia National Park, each location is unique or special in some way. The areas include other national parks, historic sites, monuments, seashores, and other recreation areas.

Each element of the National Park emblem represents something that the National Park Service protects. Fill in each blank below to show what each symbol represents.

```
WORD BANK:
_____
MOUNTAINS, ARROWHEAD, BISON,
SEQUOIA TREE, WATER
```

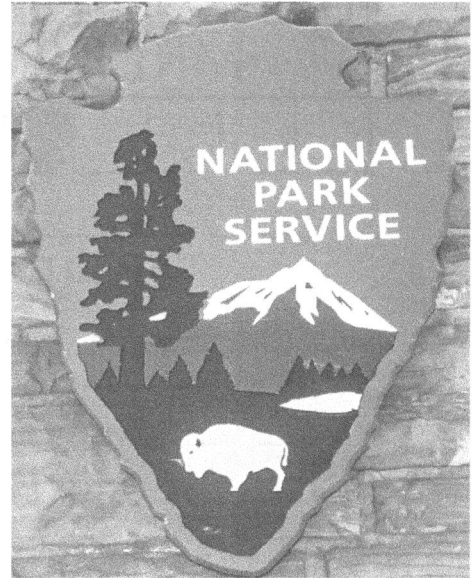

This represents all plants. _____

This represents all animals. _____

This symbol represents the landscapes. _____

This represents the waters protected by the park service. _____

This represents the historical and archeological values. _____

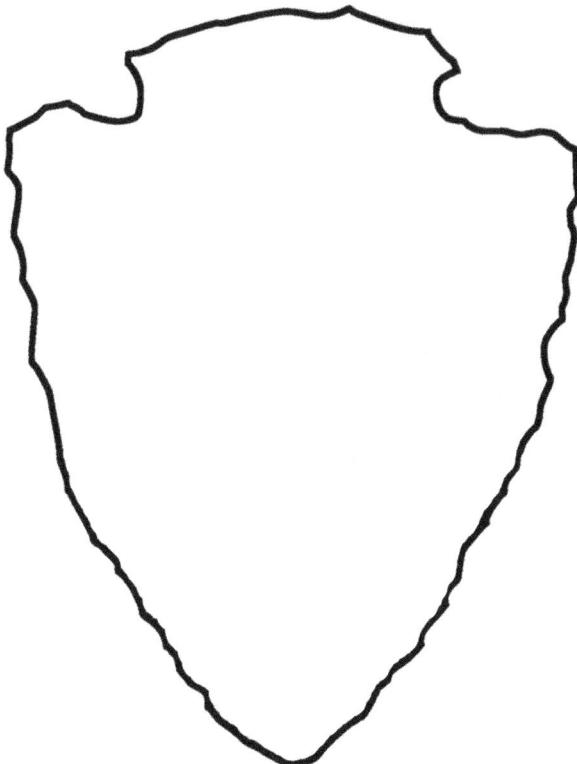

Now it's your turn! Pretend you are designing a new national park. Add elements to the design that represent the things that your park protects

What is the name of your park?

Describe why you included the symbols that you included. What do they mean?

5

Things to Do Jumble

Unscramble the letters to uncover activities you can do while in Sequoia National Park. Hint: each one ends in -ing.

1. MRLKCCOBI
   ☐☐☐☐■☐☐☐☐☐ING

2. KHI
   ☐☐☐ING

3. RDIB
   ☐☐☐☐ING

4. MACP
   ☐☐☐☐ING

5. KNICIPC
   ☐☐☐☐☐☐☐ING

6. EISSTEHG
   ☐☐☐☐☐☐☐☐ING

7. ESWHOSNO
   ☐☐☐☐☐☐☐☐ING

Word Bank

birding
reading
camping
snowshoeing
rock climbing
hiking
hunting
singing
yelling
sightseeing
picnicking

Photobook

Draw some pictures of
things you saw in the park.

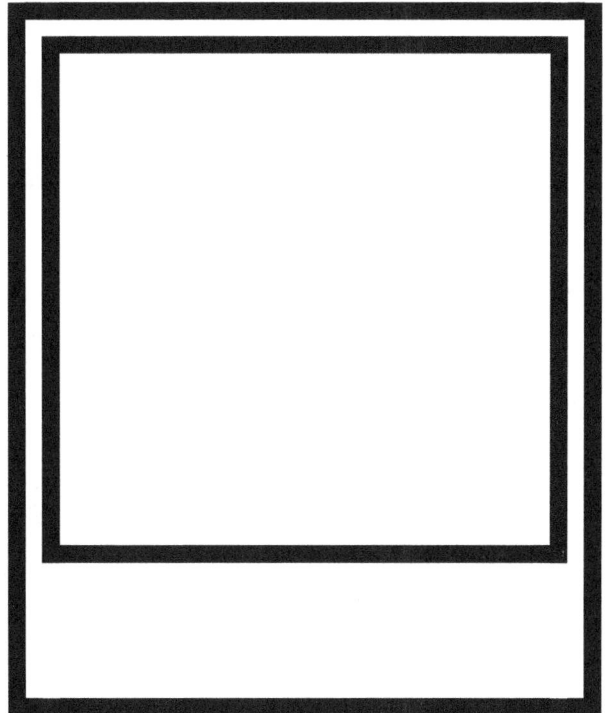

Go Birdwatching at Moro Rock

start here

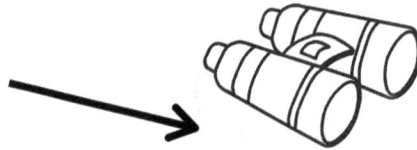

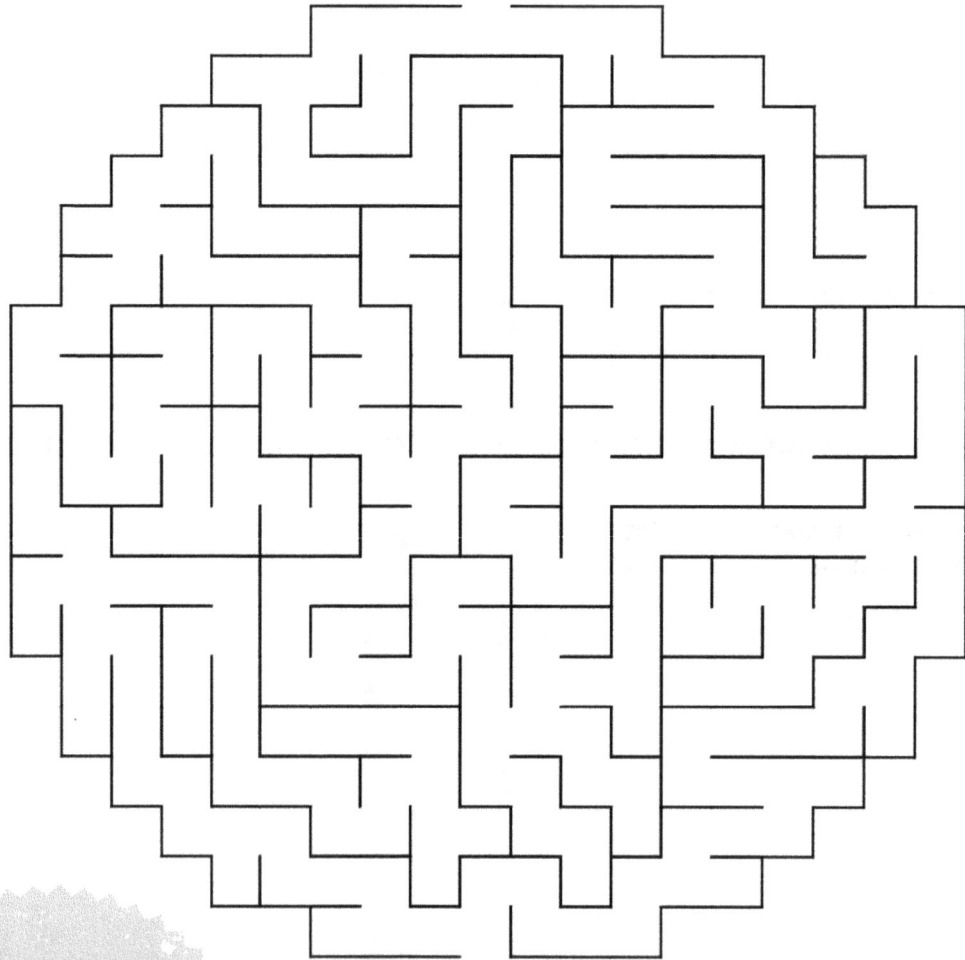

DID YOU KNOW?

Sequoia National Park is home to several birds of prey, including eagles, hawks, and owls. Birds of prey are birds that hunt other animals for food.

Camping Packing List

What should you take with you camping? Pretend you are in charge of your family camping trip. Make a list of what you would need to be safe and comfortable on an overnight excursion. Some considerations are listed on the side.

1.
2.
3.
4.
5.
6.
7.
8.
9.
10.
11.
12.
13.
14.
15.
16.

- What will you eat at every meal?

- What will the weather be like?

- Where will you sleep?

- What will you do during your free time?

- How luxurious do you want camp to be?

- How will you cook?

- How will you see at night?

- How will you dispose of trash?

- What might you need in case of emergencies?

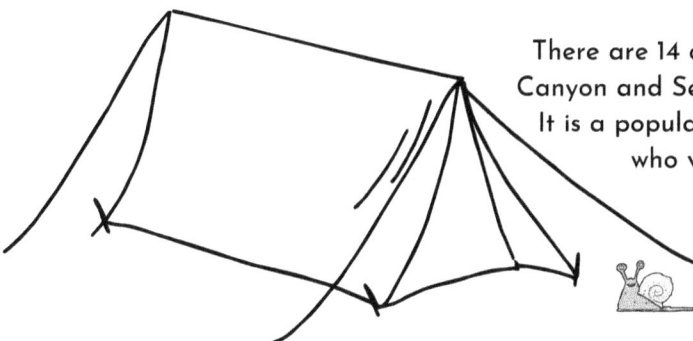

There are 14 campgrounds in Kings Canyon and Sequoia National Parks! It is a popular activity with people who visit the area.

Sequoia National Park

Date: _____

Season: _____

Who I went with: _____

Which entrance: _____

How was your experience? Write a few sentences on your trip. Where did you stay? What did you do? What was your favorite activity? If you have not yet visited the park, write a paragraph pretending that you did.

_____

_____

_____

_____

_____

STAMPS

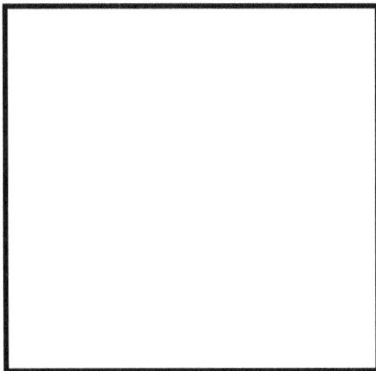

Many national parks and monuments have cancellation stamps for visitors to use. These rubber stamps record the date and the location that you visited. Many people collect the markings as a free souvenir. Check with a ranger to see where you can find a stamp during your visit. If you aren't able to find one, you can draw your own.

Where is the Park?

Sequoia National Park is in the western United States. It is located in California. There are a total of 9 national parks in California, more than any other state!

California

Look at the shape of California. Can you find it on the map? If you are from the US, can you find your home state? Color California green. Color every state that touches California blue. Put a star on the map where you live. Color the rest of the map any way you'd like.

Connect the Dots #1

Connect the dots to figure out what this tiny critter is. There are five types of these that live in Sequoia National Park.

29 1
28 2
26 27 6 7 8 11 9 10
3 5 12
4 13
25
24 23 14
15
22 16
21 17
20 18
19

Their heart rate can reach as high as 1,260 beats per minute and a breathing rate of 250 breaths per minute. Have you ever measured your breathing rate? Ask a friend or family member to set a timer for 60 seconds. Once they say "go", try to breathe normally. Count each breath until they say "stop." How do your breaths per minute compare to hummingbirds?

_____

_____

Yellow-bellied marmots are one of the few mammals that survive in the high alpine areas of the Sierras. They spend most of their time in their burrows.

The only species of bear that lives here now are black bears. California grizzlies were once abundant, but have been extinct since the 1920s.

Who lives here?

Here are eight plants and animals that live in the park.
Use the word bank to fill in the clues below.

WORD BANK: GOPHER SNAKE, QUAIL, POSSUM, MARMOT, WESTERN TOAD, PIKA, BEAVER, WILD TURKEY

☐ ☐ ☐ S ☐ ☐

☐ ☐ ☐ ☐ E ☐ ☐ ■ ☐ ☐ ☐

Q ☐ ☐ ☐ ☐

☐ ☐ ☐ ☐ ■ ☐ U ☐ ☐ ☐

☐ ☐ ☐ ☐ O ☐

☐ I ☐ ☐

☐ ☐ A ☐ ☐ ☐

☐ ☐ ☐ ☐ ☐ ☐ ■ S ☐ ☐ ☐ ☐

Porcupines are well known for their defense mechanism, their quills! If attacked, these quills easily detach from the porcupine's back to pierce potential predators.

California quail are identifiable by the plume on the top of their heads. This feature is made of 6 feathers!

Common Names
vs.
Scientific Names

A common name of an organism is a name that is based on everyday language. You have heard the common names of plants, animals, and other living things on tv, in books, and at school. Common names can also be referred to as "English" names, popular names, or farmer's name. Common names can vary from place to place. The word for a particular tree may be one thing, but that same tree has a different name in another country. Common names can even vary from region to region, even in the same country.

Scientific names, or Latin names, are given to organisms to make it possible to have uniform names for the same species. Scientific names are in Latin. You may have heard plants or animals referred to by their scientific name, or at least parts of their scientific names. Latin names are also called "binomial nomenclature" which refers to a two-part naming system. The first part of the name - the generic name –names the genus to which the species belongs. The second part of the name, the specific name, identifies the species. For example, Tyrannosaurus rex is an example of a widely known scientific name.

American Black Bear

Ursus americanus

COMMON NAME

Brewer's Blackbird

Euphagus cyanocephalus

LATIN NAME = GENUS + SPECIES

Brewer's Blackbird = Euphagus cyanocephalus

Black Bear = Ursus americanus

Find the Match!
Common Names and Latin Names

Match the common name to the scientific name for each animal. The first one is done for you. Use clues on the page before and after this one to complete the matches.

Brewer's Blackbird   Haliaeetus leucocephalus

Giant Sequoia   Ursus americanus

Corn Lily   Lagopus leucura

American Black Bear   Ochotona princeps

Great Horned Owl   Sequoiadendron giganteum

Bald Eagle   Charina bottae

Ptarmigan   Bubo virginianus

Pika   Euphagus cyanocephalus

Rubber Boa   Veratrum californicum

Bald Eagle

Haliaeetus leucocephalus

Ptarmigan
Lagopus leucura

Bald Eagle
Haliaeetus leucocephalus

Great Horned Owl
Bubo virginianus

Some plants and animals that live at Sequoia NP.

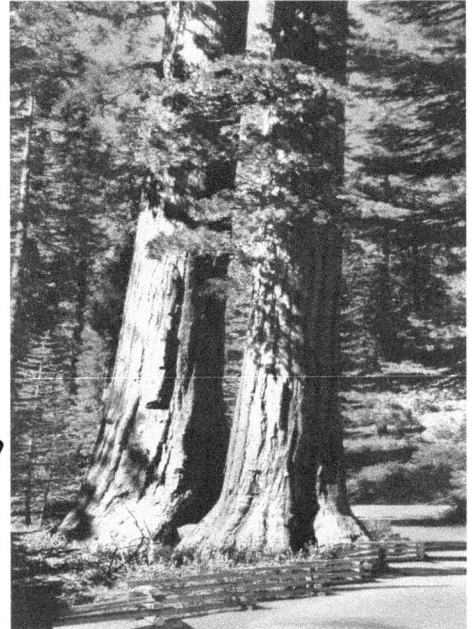

Giant Sequoia
Sequoiadendron giganteum

Pika
Ochotona princeps

Rubber Boa
Charina bottae

Wildlife Wisdom

Sequoia National Park is home to a lot of different kinds of animals. Seeing wildlife can be an exciting thing about visiting the national park but it is important to remember that these animals are wild. They need plenty of space and a healthy habitat where they can find their own food. Part of this is not allowing animals to eat any human food. This is their home and we are the visitors. We need to be respectful of the wildlife in the park.

Directions: Circle the highlighted words that best complete the following sentences.

If an animal changes its behavior because of your presence, you are **too close / funny looking / dehydrated and should drink more water.**

The best thing we can do to help wild animals survive is **make them pets / protect their habitat / knit them winter sweaters.**

In a national park it is **never / always / sometimes** okay to share your food with wild animals.

When you're hiking in an area where there are bears, you should **hike quietly / make noise / wear bright colors** to warn bears that you are entering their space.

At night, park rangers care for the animals by **putting them back into their cages / tucking them into bed / leaving them alone.**

If you see an abandoned bird's nest, it is best to **pet the baby birds / leave it alone / crunch the empty eggshells.**

Bears look under logs in hopes of finding **granola bars / insects / peanuts to eat.**

The place where an animal lives is called its **condo / habitat / crib.**

The Ten Essentials

The ten essentials is a list of things that are important to have when you go for longer hikes. If you go on a hike to the <u>backcountry</u>, it is especially important that you have everything you need in case of an emergency. If you get lost or something unforeseen happens, it is good to be prepared to survive until help finds you.

The ten essentials list was developed in the 1930s by an outdoors group called the Mountaineers. Over time and technological advancements, this list has evolved. Can you identify all the things on the current list? Circle each of the "essentials" and cross out everything that doesn't make the cut.

fire: matches, lighter, tinder and/or stove	a pint of milk	extra money	headlamp plus extra batteries	extra clothes
extra water	a dog	Polaroid camera	bug net	lightweight games, like a deck of cards
extra food	a roll of duct tape	shelter	sun protection like sunglasses, sun-protective clothes and sunscreen	knife: plus a gear repair kit
a mirror	navigation: map, compass, altimeter, GPS device, or satellite messenger	first aid kit	extra flip-flops	entertainment like video games or books

Backcountry- a remote undeveloped rural area.

Map Symbol Sudoku

The National Park System makes park maps using symbols instead of words. They are easily understood and take up way less space on a tiny map.

🚶	💧	🌲	⛺
Trailhead	Waterfall	Wilderness	Campground

Complete this symbol sudoku puzzle. Fill each square with one of the symbols. Each one can appear only once in each row, column, and mini 2x2 grid. Each symbol means something, so you can write what the symbol represents instead of drawing the symbols if you prefer.

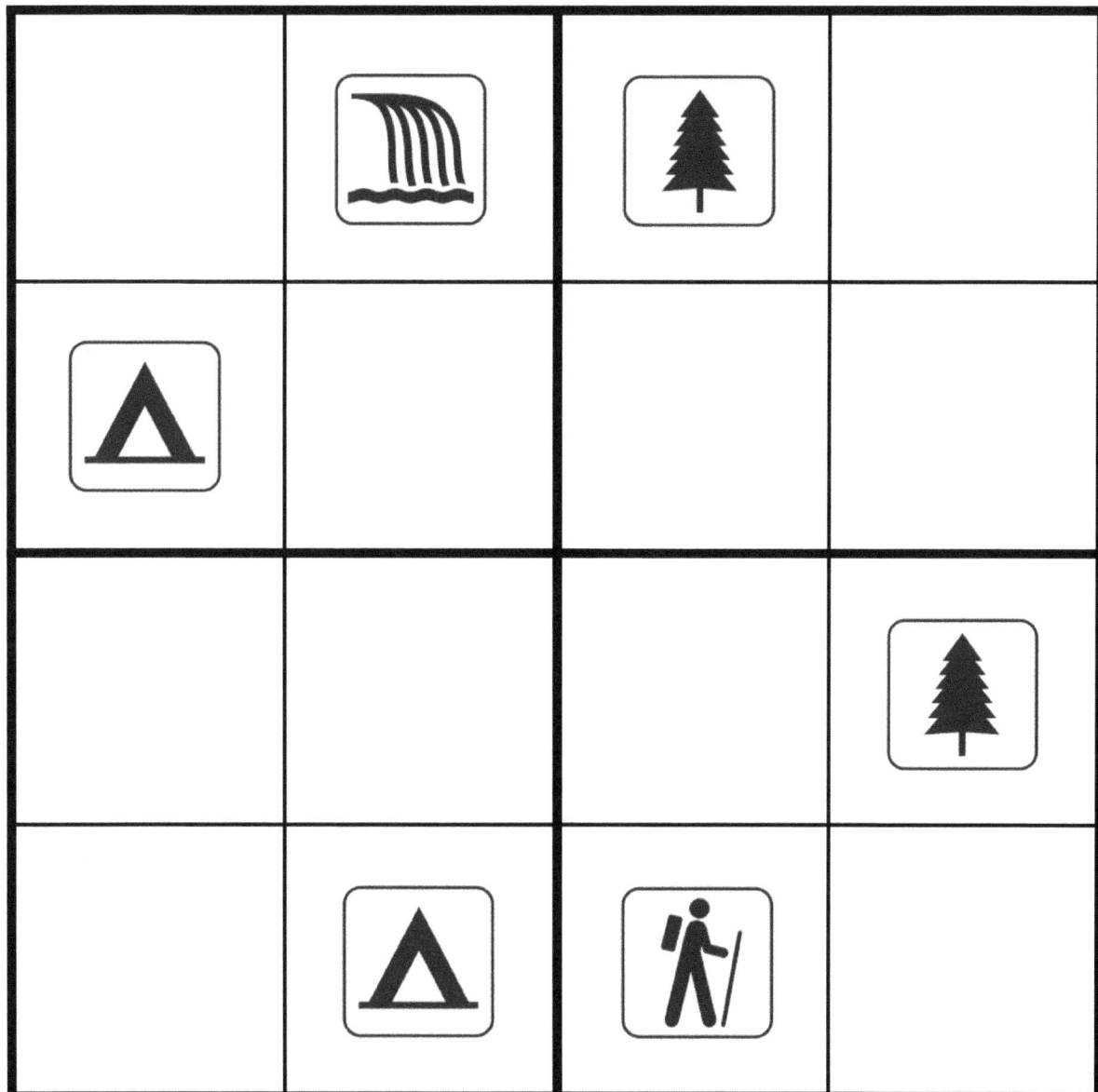

	Waterfall	Wilderness	
Campground			
			Wilderness
	Campground	Trailhead	

Connect the Dots #2

California Condors have the largest wingspan of any other bird in North America. Condors have wingspans of up to eleven feet! A wingspan is the distance from one wingtip to the other wingtip. There is a similar measurement for humans. This is called an arm span, since humans don't have wings.

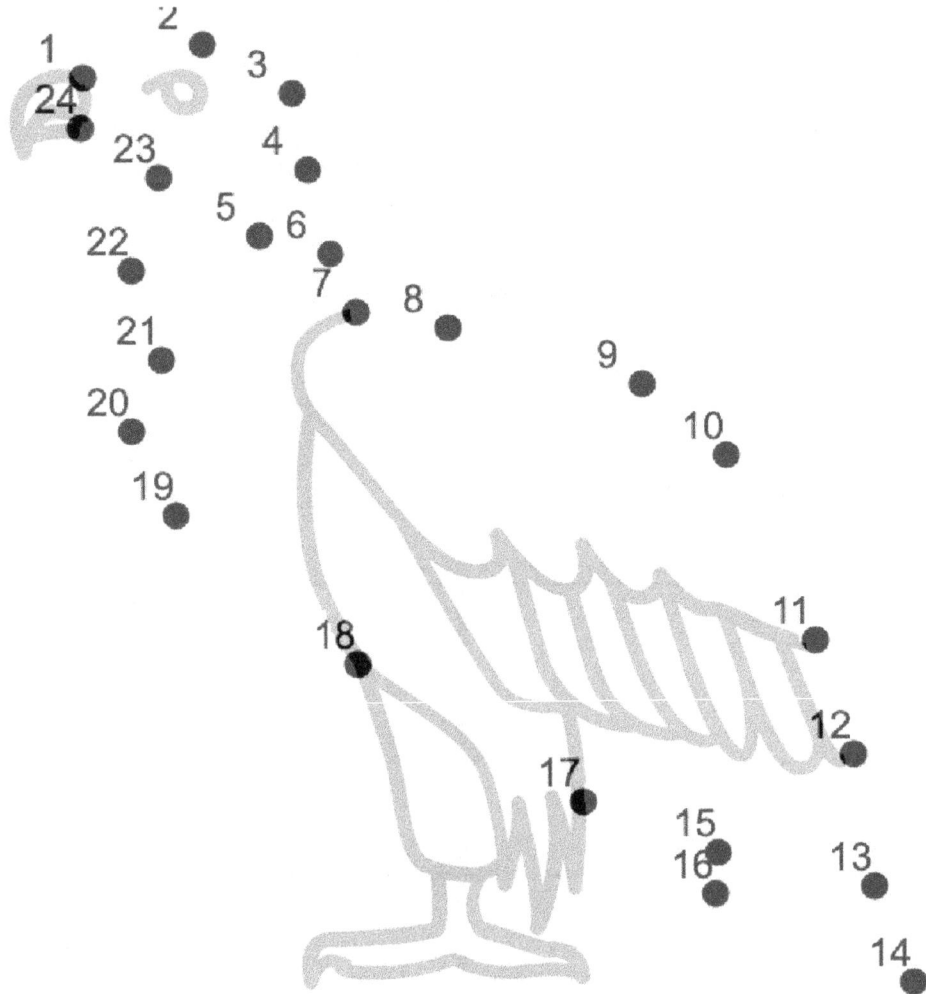

Do you know how long your arm span is? You can have a friend or family member help you measure it. Stand with your back against a wall and stretch out your arms. With a measuring tape, measure from the tip of your left middle finger to the tip of your right middle finger. How long is your arm span? Is it longer or shorter than the wingspan of a California Condor?

_____

_____

LISTEN CAREFULLY

Visitors to Sequoia National Park may hear different noises from those they hear at home. Try this activity to experience this for yourself!

First, find a place outside where it is comfortable to sit or stand for a few minutes. You can do this by yourself or with a friend or family member. Once you have a good spot, close your eyes and listen. Be quiet for one minute and pay attention to what you are hearing. List some of the sounds you have heard in one of the two boxes below:

NATURAL SOUNDS
MADE BY ANIMALS, TREES OR PLANTS, THE WIND, ETC

HUMAN-MADE SOUNDS
MADE BY PEOPLE, MACHINES, ETC

ONCE YOU ARE BACK AT HOME, TRY REPEATING YOUR EXPERIMENT:

NATURAL SOUNDS
MADE BY ANIMALS, TREES OR PLANTS, THE WIND, ETC

HUMAN-MADE SOUNDS
MADE BY PEOPLE, MACHINES, ETC

WHERE DID YOU HEAR MORE NATURAL SOUNDS? _____

WHERE DID YOU HEAR MORE HUMAN SOUNDS? _____

Sound Exploration

Spend a minute or two listening to all of the sounds around you.
Draw your favorite sound.

How did this sound make you feel?

_____

_____

What did you think when you heard this sound?

_____

_____

Sequoia Word Search

Words may be horizontal, vertical, or diagonal
and they might be backward!

1. giant sequoia
2. trees
3. forest
4. black bear
5. Moro Rock
6. Tunnel Tree
7. meadow
8. coyote
9. streams
10. California
11. cedar grove
12. pinecones
13. marble
14. Crystal Cave
15. pikas
16. marmot
17. skunk
18. wildfire

```
G W I L D F I R E F O R E S T
H I B A S I L S T R E A M S U
M E A D O W O S C E L B O P N
S P I N E C O N E S R L R A N
C E A D T A B L O N I U O N E
A T R E E S C O Y O T E R O L
L E E T E H E K I N K R O R T
I L V A M B I Q G W N E C A R
F E A S G L L O U E I D K M E
O C C E D A R G R O V E O I E
R T L H C C I N O O I E M C N
N R A I K K E I S M O A I P E
I I T S H B I R E I R A L O W
A C S O L E V E S B S A K I P
N I Y K K A I N L R E L H N A
X T R F U R E E L Z Q S Q T L
H Y C R O N L E C T U I C E E
B R I A N N K D N T O M R A M
```

25

Bear Aware

Bears in the wild have plenty of things to eat! When you are in bear country, it is especially important to keep bears safe by making sure they can't eat any human food. When you are camping, you should store your food in special bear boxes. These metal storage boxes are animal-proof and will prevent wildlife from getting to your food.

Draw a line from each item to either the bear (if it is safe for bears to eat it) or to the bear box (if it needs to be stored.)

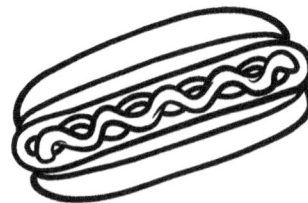

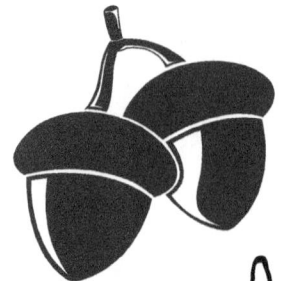

Protecting the Park

When you visit national parks, it is important to leave the park the way you found it. Did you know that the national parks get hundreds of millions of visitors every year? We can only protect national parks for future visitors to enjoy if everyone does their part. The choices that each visitor makes when visiting the park have a big impact all together.

Read each line below. Write a sentence or draw a picture to show the impacts these changes would make on the park.

What would happen if every visitor fed the wild animals?

What would happen if every visitor picked a flower?

What would happen if every visitor took home a few rocks?

What would happen if every visitor wrote or carved their name on the rocks or trees?

The Perfect Picnic Spot

Fill in the blanks on this page without looking at the full story. Once you have each line filled out, use the words you've chosen to complete the story on the next page.

EMOTION _____

FOOD _____

SOMETHING SWEET _____

STORE _____

MODE OF TRANSPORTATION _____

NOUN _____

SOMETHING ALIVE _____

SAUCE _____

PLURAL VEGETABLES _____

ADJECTIVE _____

PLURAL BODY PART _____

ANIMAL _____

PLURAL FRUIT _____

PLACE _____

SOMETHING TALL _____

COLOR _____

ADJECTIVE _____

NOUN _____

A DIFFERENT ANIMAL _____

FAMILY MEMBER #1 _____

FAMILY MEMBER #2 _____

VERB THAT ENDS IN -ING _____

A DIFFERENT FOOD _____

The Perfect Picnic Spot

Use the words from the previous page to complete a silly story.

When my family suggested having our lunch at the Mineral King campground, I

was _____. I love eating my _____ outside! I knew we had picked up a
    EMOTION   FOOD

box of _____ from the _____ for after lunch, my favorite. We drove up
    SOMETHING SWEET   STORE

to the area and I jumped out of the _____. "I will find the perfect spot for
                                    MODE OF TRANSPORTATION

a picnic!" I grabbed a _____ for us to sit on, and I ran off. I passed a picnic
                       NOUN

table, but it was covered with _____ so we couldn't sit there. The next
                               SOMETHING ALIVE

picnic table looked okay, but there were smears of _____ and pieces of
                                                   SAUCE

_____ everywhere. The people that were there before must have been
PLURAL VEGETABLES

_____! I gritted my _____ together and kept walking down the path,
ADJECTIVE   PLURAL BODY PART

determined to find the perfect spot. I wanted a table with a good view of the

waterfall. Why was this so hard? If we were lucky, I might even get to see

_____ eating some _____ on the cliffside. They don't have those in
ANIMAL   PLURAL FRUIT

_____ where I am from. I walked down a little hill and there it was, the
PLACE

perfect spot! The trees towered overhead and looked as tall as _____. The
                                                               SOMETHING TALL

patch of grass was a beautiful _____ color. The _____ flowers were
                               COLOR   ADJECTIVE

growing on the side of a _____. I looked across the waterfall and even saw a
                         NOUN

_____ on the edge of a rock. I looked back to see my _____ and
DIFFERENT ANIMAL   FAMILY MEMBER #1

_____ _____ a picnic basket. "I hope you brought plenty of
FAMILY MEMBER #2   VERB THAT ENDS IN ING

_____, I'm starving!"
A DIFFERENT FOOD

29

Hike to see the Giant Sequoias

start here

DID YOU KNOW?

The General Sherman tree in Kings Canyon National Park is the largest tree in the world by volume.

The Biggest Trees
Word Search

Giant Sequoias are some of the biggest trees in the world. Many of the very largest trees are named and closely monitored. These are some of the biggest ones in Kings Canyon and Sequoia National Park. Can you find them?

1. General Sherman
2. General Grant
3. President
4. Lincoln
5. Stagg
6. Boole
7. Genesis
8. Franklin
9. Monroe
10. Column
11. Euclid
12. Pershing
13. Diamond
14. Adams
15. Nelder
16. Hart

```
G D E S C A N Y O N D E D W C
E E D P M I F R A N K L I N H
N V N R K I T E A W A L A O A
E E U E H A R T U Y U T M M T
S N N S R D Y P L C Y R O K R
I P D I Y A R E C T L E N O E
S O S D P M L R R H L I D A E
A R B E M S I S D I L S D N G
L T H N G I L H H N U D E C E
S I S T A G G I K E U G R O R
E S N U A E I N N L R B N L N
Q H N C K N O G S D S M T U E
U J O S O E I N Z E I O A M C
O Y G E L L V E I R D N V N O
I W E L D A N A D O A R H E M
A T G E N E R E N L B O O L E
U A E E S A E N N O A E V E B
C G E N E R A L G R A N T O N
```

31

Leave No Trace Quiz

Leave No Trace is a concept that helps people make decisions during outdoor recreation that protects the environment. There are seven principles that guide us when we spend time outdoors, whether you are in a national park or not. Are you an expert in Leave No Trace? Take this quiz and find out!

1. How can you plan ahead and prepare to ensure you have the best experience you can in the national park?
   a. Make sure you stop by the ranger station for a map and to ask about current conditions.
   b. Just wing it! You will know the best trail when you see it.
   c. Stick to your plan, even if conditions change. You traveled a long way to get here, and you should stick to your plan.
2. What is an example of traveling on a durable surface?
   a. Walking only on the designated path.
   b. Walking on the grass that borders the trail if the trail is very muddy.
   c. Taking a shortcut if you can find one since it means you will be walking less.
3. Why should you dispose of waste properly?
   a. You don't need to. Park rangers love to pick up the trash you leave behind.
   b. You actually should leave your leftovers behind, because animals will eat them. It is important to make sure they aren't hungry.
   c. So that other peoples' experiences of the park are not impacted by you leaving your waste behind.
4. How can you best follow the concept "leave what you find"?
   a. Take only a small rock or leaf to remember your trip.
   b. Take pictures, but leave any physical items where they are.
   c. Leave everything you find, unless it may be rare like an arrowhead, then it is okay to take.
5. What is not a good example of minimizing campfire impacts?
   a. Only having a campfire in a pre-existing campfire ring.
   b. Checking in with current conditions when you consider making a campfire.
   c. Building a new campfire ring in a location that has a better view.
6. What is a poor example of respecting wildlife?
   a. Building squirrel houses out of rocks so the squirrels have a place to live.
   b. Stay far away from wildlife and give them plenty of space.
   c. Reminding your grown-ups to not drive too fast in animal habitats while visiting the park.
7. How can you show consideration of other visitors?
   a. Play music on your speaker so other people at the campground can enjoy it.
   b. Wear headphones on the trail if you choose to listen to music.
   c. Make sure to yell "Hello!" to every animal you see at top volume.

Park Poetry

America's parks inspire art of all kinds. Painters, sculptors, photographers, writers, and artists of all mediums have taken inspiration from natural beauty. They have turned their inspiration into great works.

Use this space to write your own poem about the park. Think about what you have experienced or seen. Use descriptive language to create an acrostic poem. This type of poem has the first letter of each line spell out another word. Create an acrostic that spells out the word "Forest."

F _____

O _____

R _____

E _____

S _____

T _____

F orests so tall
O ver the mountains
R ushing river
E ach tree so big
S equoias
T ell everyone how cool

F resh and early
O nly us on the road
R eady to sled
E ach mitten on
S now everywhere!
T reats to warm up

When Nature Calls...

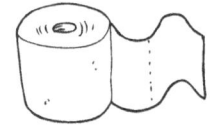

Read the following paragraph to discover the important waste management plays in our national parks. Fill in the blanks with words from the word bank, at right, as you read.

Word Bank:

flush

flow

hard

urinate

ecosystem

pit

never

ashes

plumbing

container

inches

recycling

The people who work at national parks are responsible for ensuring proper waste management from guests. Waste management isn't just about making sure trash and _____ go to the right places. It also means human waste! It may not be pleasant to think about, but all humans _____ (pee) and defecate (poop). It is important to consider how to deal with human waste to keep parks clean, safe, and with as little disturbance to the _____ as possible.

There are different types of bathrooms or methods used to deal with human waste. In visitor centers, you are likely to encounter a standard _____ toilet, which uses water and modern _____ to whisk your waste away. Near trails or at campgrounds, you may find toilets that don't flush. A _____ toilet is a type of toilet built over a hole in the ground. A composting toilet decomposes human waste into compost with an aerobic process. A vault toilet stores urine and feces in an underground _____ or vault before it is pumped out. Unlike pit toilets, they are less stinky because of vent pipes, which allow air to _____ from the vault out through the ceiling.

No matter which type of toilet you encounter, there are some things you should keep in mind to help protect the park. First, _____ put anything in the toilet other than pee, poop, or toilet paper. Things like snack wrappers, diapers, or _____ from a campfire can damage toilet systems. It can cost a lot of money and time to fix. Make sure trash goes in the trash can, not any toilet.

If you have to "go" while you are in the backcountry, here is what you should do. If you have to pee, try to urinate on a _____ surface like rocks, not plants. Animals are attracted to the salt in urine and may dig up vegetation to get to it. If you have to poop, you will need to dig a cat hole. First, select a location. It must be at least 200 feet away from any water source. Use a small shovel to dig a hole about 6 _____ deep. Do your business in the hole, then bury ONLY your poop. Take a trash bag with you, as you will need to take your toilet paper with you along with the rest of your trash. If not, animals may dig up the toilet paper which is bad for them.

No matter where you go, don't forget to wash your hands with soap and water afterward! At the very least, pack hand sanitizer to use.

Catch a Fish in the Kaweah River

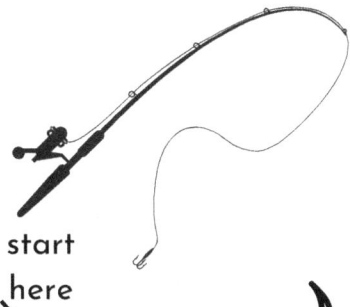

start here

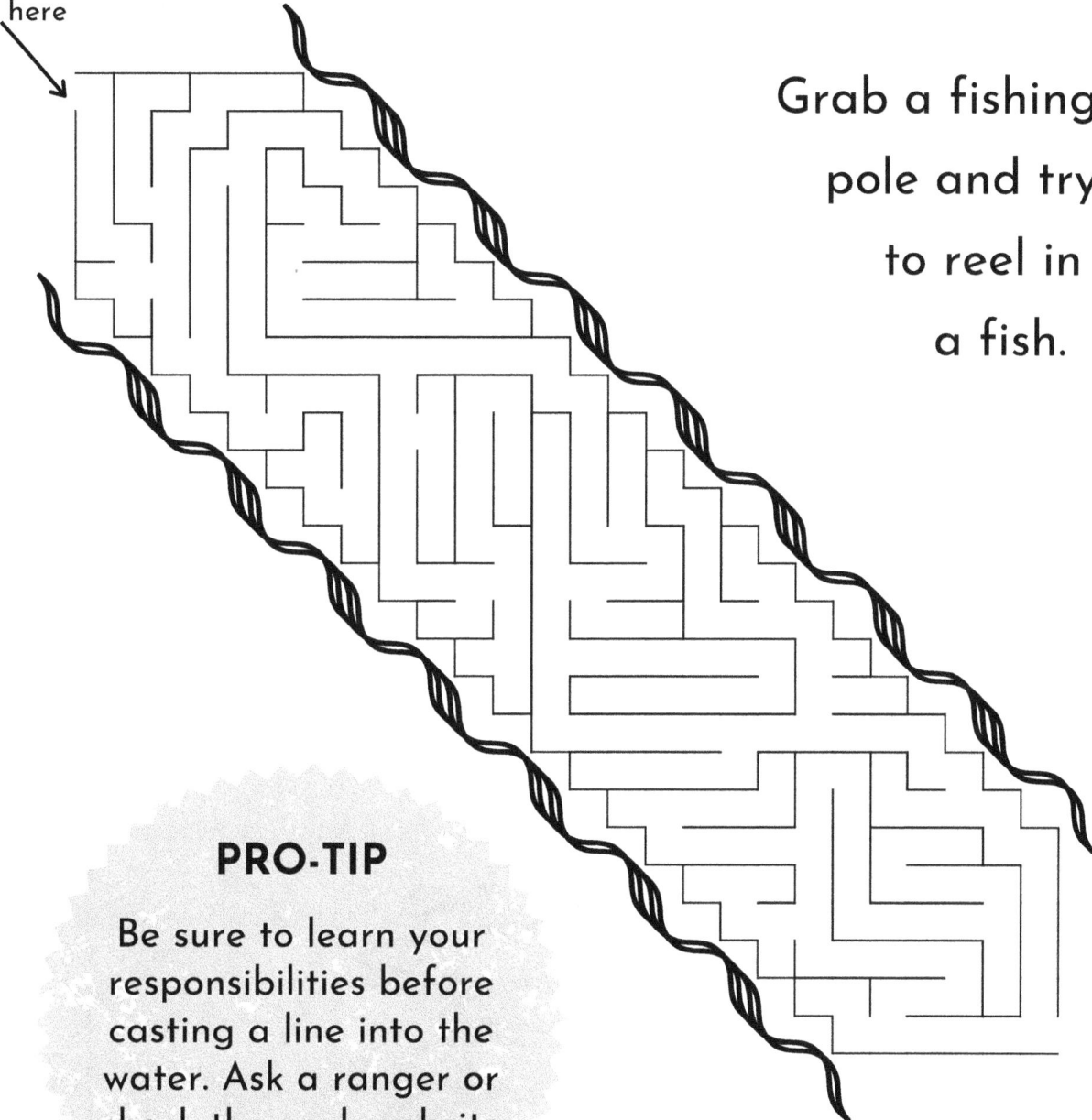

Grab a fishing pole and try to reel in a fish.

PRO-TIP

Be sure to learn your responsibilities before casting a line into the water. Ask a ranger or check the park website before you go.

Stacking Rocks

Have you ever seen stacks of rocks while hiking in national parks? Do you know what they are or what they mean? These rock piles are called cairns and often mark hiking routes in parks. Every park has a different way to maintain trails and cairns. However, they all have the same rule: If you come across a cairn, do not disturb it.

Color the cairn and the rules to remember.

1. Do not tamper with cairns.

If a cairn is tampered with or an unauthorized one is built, then future visitors may become disoriented or even lost.

2. Do not build unauthorized cairns.

Moving rocks disturbs the soil and makes the area more prone to erosion. Disturbing rocks can disturb fragile plants.

3. Do not add to existing cairns.

Authorized cairns are carefully designed. Adding to them can actually cause them to collapse.

Decoding Using American Sign Language

American Sign Language, also called ASL for short, is a language that many people who are deaf or hard of hearing use to communicate. People use ASL to communicate with their hands. Did you know people from all over the country and world travel to national parks? You may hear people speaking other languages. You might also see people using ASL. Use the American Manual Alphabet chart to decode some national parks facts.

This was the first national park to be established:

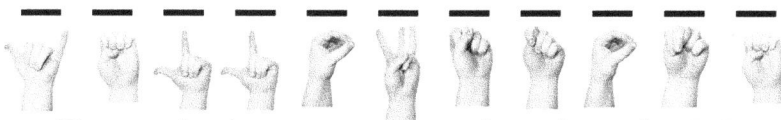

__ __ __ __ __ __ __ __ __ __ __

This is the biggest national park in the US:

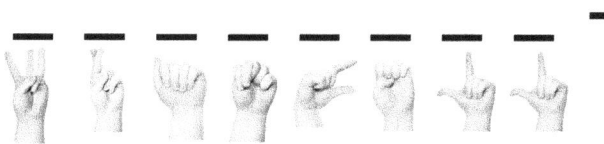

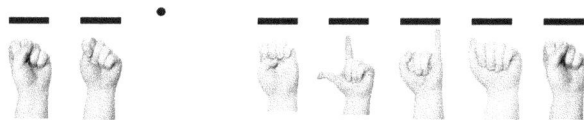

__ __ __ __ __ __ __ -

__ __ . __ __ __ __ __

This is the most visited national park:

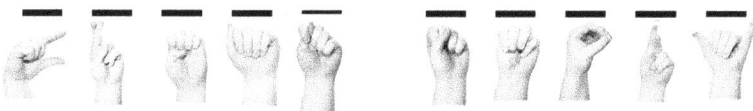

__ __ __ __ __ __ __ __

__ __ __ __ __ __ __ __

Aa	Bb	Cc	Dd	Ee
Ff	Gg		Hh	Ii
Jj	Kk	Ll	Mm	Nn
Oo	Pp	Qq		Rr
Ss	Tt	Uu		Vv
Ww	Xx	Yy	Zz	

Hint: Pay close attention to the position of the thumb!

Try it! Using the chart, try to make the letters of the alphabet with your hand. What is the hardest letter to make? Can you spell out your name? Show a friend or family member and have them watch you spell out the name of the national park you are in.

Go Horseback Riding to the Sequoia Grove

Help find the horse's lost shoe!

start here

DID YOU KNOW?

Horseback riding is a popular activity in Sequoia National Park. There are many trails that you can take horses for day trips.

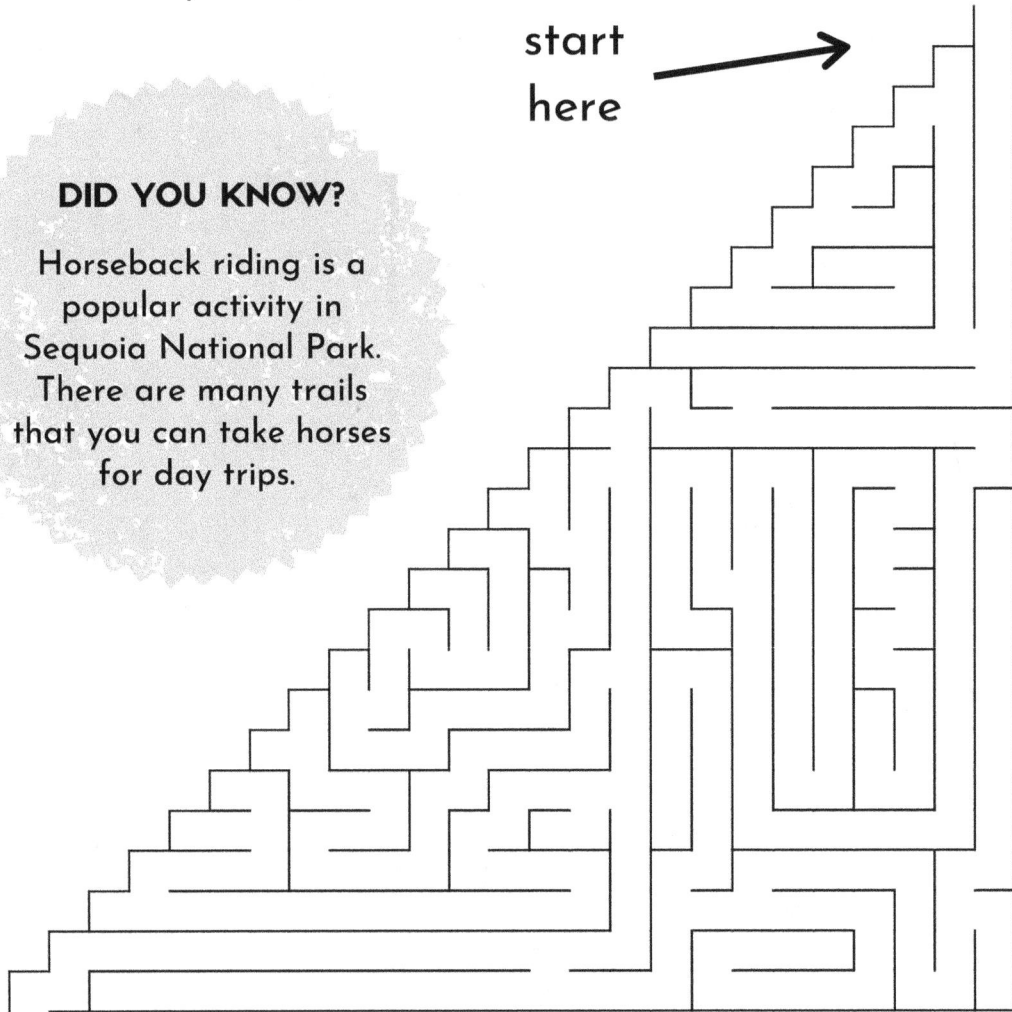

Butterflies of the Sierras

Dozens of species of butterflies and moths live in Sequoia National Park. Their wingspan size varies, as do the patterns on their wings. Design your own butterfly below. Make sure the wings are symmetrical, meaning both sides match.

A Hike at Timber Gap

Fill in the blanks on this page without looking at the full story. Once you have each line filled out, use the words you've chosen to complete the story on the next page.

ADJECTIVE _____

SOMETHING TO EAT _____

SOMETHING TO DRINK _____

NOUN _____

ARTICLE OF CLOTHING _____

BODY PART _____

VERB _____

ANIMAL _____

SAME TYPE OF FOOD _____

ADJECTIVE _____

SAME ANIMAL _____

VERB THAT ENDS IN "ED" _____

NUMBER _____

A DIFFERENT NUMBER _____

SOMETHING THAT FLIES _____

LIGHT SOURCE _____

PLURAL NOUN _____

FAMILY MEMBER _____

YOUR NICKNAME _____

A Hike at Timber Gap

Use the words from the previous page to complete a silly story.

I went for a hike at Timber Gap today. In my favorite _ _ _ _ _ _ backpack, I
ADJECTIVE

made sure to pack a map so I wouldn't get lost. I also threw in an extra

_ _ _ _ _ _ _ _ _ _ just in case I got hungry and a bottle of _ _ _ _ _ _ _ _ _ _. I put
SOMETHING TO EAT   SOMETHING TO DRINK

on my _ _ _ _ _ _ _ _ _ spray, and a tied a _ _ _ _ _ _ _ _ _ _ _ around my
       NOUN   ARTICLE OF CLOTHING

_ _ _ _ _ _ _ _ _, in case it gets chilly. I started to _ _ _ _ _ _ down the path. As
BODY PART   VERB

soon as I turned the corner, I came face to face with a(n) _ _ _ _ _ _ _ _. I think
                                                           ANIMAL

it was as startled as I was! What should I do? I had to think fast! Should I

give it some of my _ _ _ _ _ _ _ _ _ _ _? No. I had to remember what the
                   SAME TYPE OF FOOD

_ _ _ _ _ _ _ ranger told me. "If you see one, back away slowly and try not to
ADJECTIVE

scare it." Soon enough, the _ _ _ _ _ _ _ _ _ _   _ _ _ _ _ _ _ _ _ _ away. The coast
                            SAME ANIMAL   VERB THAT ENDS IN ED

was clear. _ _ _ _ _ _ hours later, I finally got to the lookout. I felt like I could
           NUMBER

see for a _ _ _ _ _ _ miles. I took a picture of a _ _ _ _ _ _ _ _ so I could always
          A DIFFERENT NUMBER   NOUN

remember this moment. As I was putting my camera away, a _ _ _ _ _ _ _ _ _
                                                          SOMETHING THAT FLIES

flew by, reminding me that it was almost nighttime. I turned on my

_ _ _ _ _ _ _ _ _ and headed back. I could hear the _ _ _ _ _ _ _ _ _ _ singing their
LIGHT SOURCE   PLURAL INSECT

evening song. Just as I was getting tired, I saw my _ _ _ _ _ _ _ _ _ and our tent.
                                                    FAMILY MEMBER

"Welcome back _ _ _ _ _ _ _! How was your hike?"
              NICKNAME

41

Snail Mail

Design a postcard to send to a friend or a family member. Who do you want to tell about Sequoia National Park? In the first template, write your message. In the second template, create a design for the front of the postcard. You could show something you saw, something you did, or something you want to do in the national park.

Postcard

Camping at Buckeye Flat
Word Search

Words may be horizontal, vertical, or diagonal and they might be backward!

1. tent
2. camp stove
3. sleeping bag
4. bug spray
5. sunscreen
6. map
7. flashlight
8. pillow
9. lantern
10. ice
11. snacks
12. smores
13. water
14. first aid kit
15. chair
16. cards
17. books
18. games
19. trail
20. hat

```
D P P I L L O W D B T E A C I
E O A D P R E A A M B R C A N
P W C A M P S T O V E I H X G
R A H S G E L E B E E D A P S
E L B U G S P R A Y N G I E A
S I A H G C I C N N M E R C N
C W N L A F I R S K O O B F K
M T A E M I L E L H M R W L J
T A P R E A O R E S L B A A B
S M P A S R R T E N T L U S C
C E A I I R C G P E I U J H A
S S N A C K S S I M O K I L R
I J R S F O I S N J R A Q I D
C Y E T L E V E G U O R V G S
E W T A K C A B B S S O H H M
X J N F I R S T A I D K I T T
U A A E S S E N G E T P V A B
C J L I A R T D N A M A H A S
```

43

All in the Day of a Park Ranger

Park Rangers are hardworking individuals dedicated to protecting our parks, monuments, museums, and more. They take care of the natural and cultural resources for future generations. Rangers also help protect the visitors of the park. Their responsibilities are broad and they work both with the public and behind the scenes.

What have you seen park rangers do? Use your knowledge of the duties of park rangers to fill out a typical daily schedule, one activity for each hour. Feel free to make up your own, but some examples of activities are provided on the right. Read carefully, not all of the example activities are befitting a ranger!

Time	Activity		Examples
6 am	Lead a sunrise hike	•	feed the bald eagles
7 am		•	build trails for visitors to enjoy
8 am		•	throw rocks off the side of the mountain
9 am		•	rescue lost hikers
10 am		•	study animal behavior
		•	record air quality data
11 am		•	answer questions at the visitor center
		•	pick wildflowers
		•	pick up litter
12 pm	Enjoy a lunch break outside	•	share marshmallows with squirrels
		•	repair handrails
1 pm		•	lead a class on a field trip
2 pm		•	catch frogs and make them race
3 pm		•	lead people on educational hikes
4 pm	Teach visitors about the geology of the mountains	•	write articles for the park website
5 pm		•	protect the river from pollution
6 pm		•	remove non-native plants from the park
		•	study how climate change is affecting the park
7 pm		•	give a talk about mountain lions
8 pm		•	lead a program for campers on marmots
9 pm			

If you were a park ranger, which of the above tasks would you enjoy most?

_____

Draw Yourself as a Park Ranger

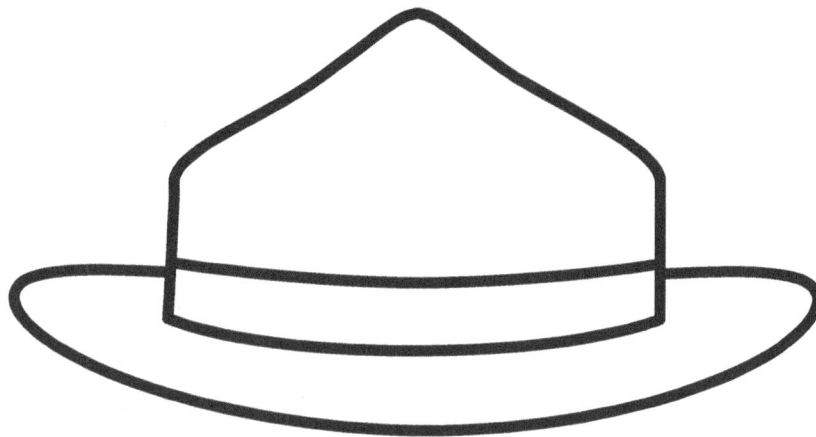

RANGER

_____

The Giant Sequoias of the Sierra Nevadas

Uh oh! The names of these famous giant sequoias got mixed up! Unscramble the letters in each circle to figure out their names!

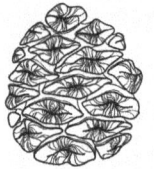

2.
REL DEN

1.
ERO NOM

5.
EGEN ISS

3.
LE BOO

4.
LRIN ANFK

1. _____

2. _____

3. _____

4. _____

5. _____

Word Bank

Monroe
Genesis
Boole
Stagg
Adam
Nelder
Hart
Franklin

Amphibians

Two species of toad and four species of frogs live in Sequoia National Park. Even more types of salamanders live there too. Frogs and toads both spend the beginning of their lives the same way, as tadpoles. Tadpoles hatch from eggs in water, usually in springs or pools of water.

Both frogs and toads are amphibians. Salamanders are amphibians too. Color the amphibians below.

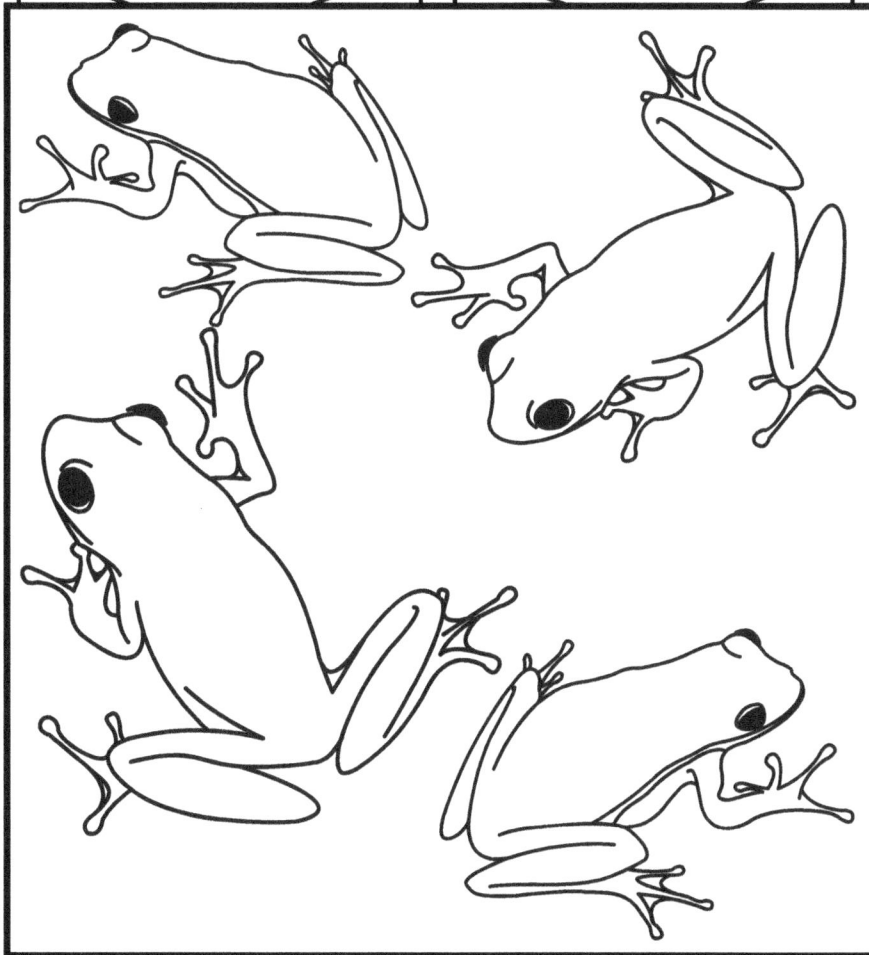

Being Respectful

Rangers need your help! Some people toss their trash where they shouldn't, create graffiti, or take artifacts when they visit Sequoia National Park. Create a poster to help show other visitors how to be respectful in the space below.

Bird Scavenger Hunt

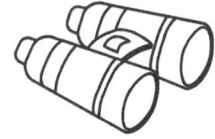

Sequoia National Park is a great place to go birdwatching. You don't have to be able to identify different species of birds in order to have fun. Open your eyes and tune in your ears. Check off as many birds on this list as you can.

☐ A colorful bird   ☐ A big bird

☐ A brown bird   ☐ A small bird

☐ A bird in a tree   ☐ A hopping bird

☐ A bird with long tail feathers   ☐ A flying bird

☐ A bird making noise   ☐ A bird's nest

☐ A bird eating or hunting   ☐ A bird's footprint on the ground

☐ A bird with spots   ☐ A bird with stripes somewhere on it

What was the easiest bird on the list to find? What was the hardest? Why do you think that was?

_____

_____

_____

63 National Parks

How many other national parks have you been to? Which one do you want to visit next? Note that some of these parks fall on the border of more than one state, you may check it off more than once!

Alaska
- [ ] Denali National Park
- [ ] Gates of the Arctic National Park
- [ ] Glacier Bay National Park
- [ ] Katmai National Park
- [ ] Kenai Fjords National Park
- [ ] Kobuk Valley National Park
- [ ] Lake Clark National Park
- [ ] Wrangell-St. Elias National Park

American Samoa
- [ ] National Park of American Samoa

Arizona
- [ ] Grand Canyon National Park
- [ ] Petrified Forest National Park
- [ ] Saguaro National Park

Arkansas
- [ ] Hot Springs National Park

California
- [ ] Channel Islands National Park
- [ ] Death Valley National Park
- [ ] Joshua Tree National Park
- [ ] Kings Canyon National Park
- [ ] Lassen Volcanic National Park
- [ ] Pinnacles National Park
- [ ] Redwood National Park
- [ ] Sequoia National Park
- [ ] Yosemite National Park

Colorado
- [ ] Black Canyon of the Gunnison National Park
- [ ] Great Sand Dunes National Park
- [ ] Mesa Verde National Park
- [ ] Rocky Mountain National Park

Florida
- [ ] Biscayne National Park
- [ ] Dry Tortugas National Park
- [ ] Everglades National Park

Hawaii
- [ ] Haleakalā National Park
- [ ] Hawai'i Volcanoes National Park

Idaho
- [ ] Yellowstone National Park

Kentucky
- [ ] Mammoth Cave National Park

Indiana
- [ ] Indiana Dunes National Park

Maine
- [ ] Acadia National Park

Michigan
- [ ] Isle Royale National Park

Minnesota
- [ ] Voyageurs National Park

Missouri
- [ ] Gateway Arch National Park

Montana
- [ ] Glacier National Park
- [ ] Yellowstone National Park

Nevada
- [ ] Death Valley National Park
- [ ] Great Basin National Park

New Mexico
- [ ] Carlsbad Caverns National Park
- [ ] White Sands National Park

North Dakota
- [ ] Theodore Roosevelt National Park

North Carolina
- [ ] Great Smoky Mountains National Park

Ohio
- [ ] Cuyahoga Valley National Park

Oregon
- [ ] Crater Lake National Park

South Carolina
- [ ] Congaree National Park

South Dakota
- [ ] Badlands National Park
- [ ] Wind Cave National Park

Tennessee
- [ ] Great Smoky Mountains National Park

Texas
- [ ] Big Bend National Park
- [ ] Guadalupe Mountains National Park

Utah
- [ ] Arches National Park
- [ ] Bryce Canyon National Park
- [ ] Canyonlands National Park
- [ ] Capitol Reef National Park
- [ ] Zion National Park

Virgin Islands
- [ ] Virgin Islands National Park

Virginia
- [ ] Shenandoah National Park

Washington
- [ ] Mount Rainier National Park
- [ ] North Cascades National Park
- [ ] Olympic National Park

West Virginia
- [ ] New River Gorge National Park

Wyoming
- [ ] Grand Teton National Park
- [ ] Yellowstone National Park

Other National Parks

Besides Sequoia National Park, there are 62 other diverse and beautiful national parks across the United States. Try your hand at this crossword. If you need help, look at the previous page for some hints.

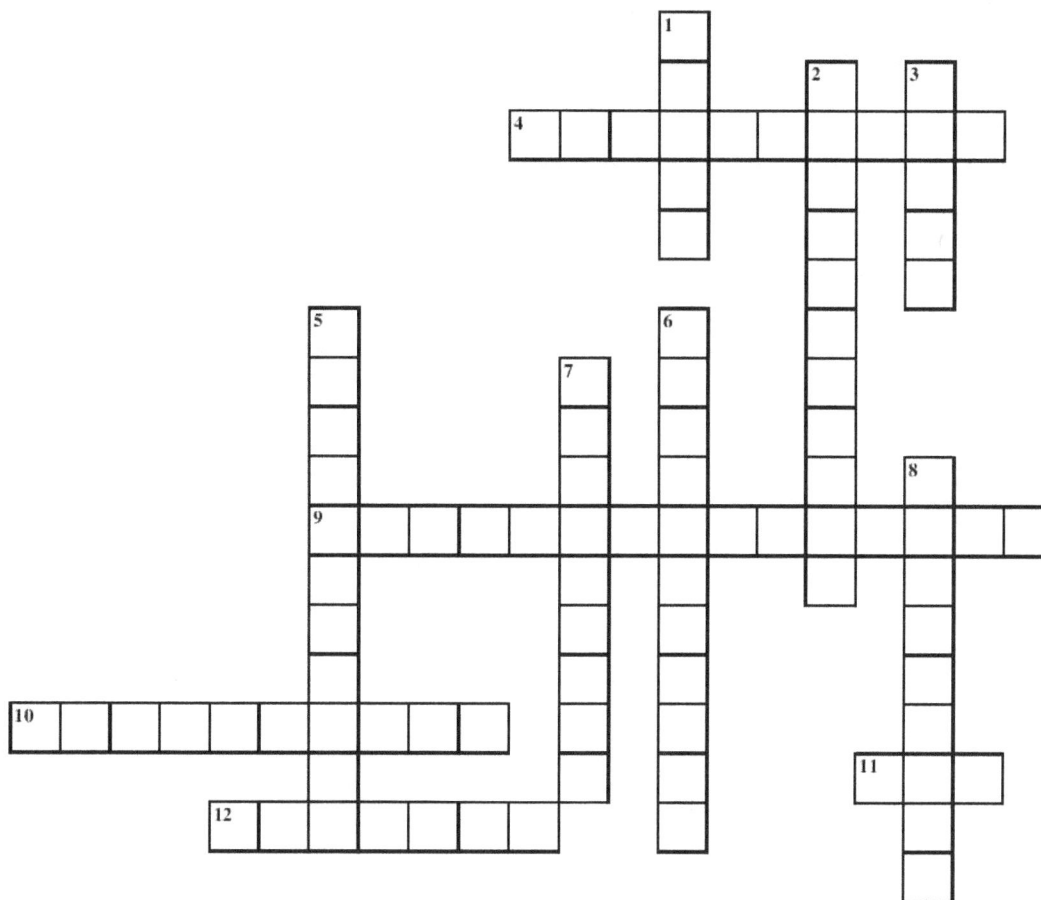

Down

1. State where Acadia National Park is located
2. This national park has the Spanish word for turtle in it.
3. Number of national parks in Alaska
5. This national park has some of the hottest temperatures in the world.
6. This national park is the only one in Idaho.
7. This toothsome creature can be famously found in Everglades National Park.
8. Only president with a national park named for them

Across

4. This state has the most national parks.
9. This park has some of the newest land in the US, caused by volcanic eruptions.
10. This park has the deepest lake in the United States.
11. This color shows up in the name of a national park in California.
12. This national park deserves a gold medal.

Which National Park Will You Go to Next?
Word Search

1. Zion
2. Big Bend
3. Glacier
4. Olympic
5. Sequoia
6. Bryce
7. Mesa Verde
8. Biscayne
9. Wind Cave
10. Great Basin
11. Katmai
12. Yellowstone
13. Voyageurs
14. Arches
15. Badlands
16. Denali
17. Glacier Bay
18. Hot Springs

```
F M M E S A V E R D E B N E Y
E A B I G B E N D E S A S E M
Y L I C A L O Y N E E D L T G
D M G A S S A U C N R L U E R
C E L I I T S C R E O A A K E
S N A W Y E E O I W T N A C A
G I C H A A Q C S E M D N S T
N O I Z P R U T I M R S N E B
I W E L M P O N B W E B K H A
R J R F D N I F L I H B U C S
P A B E E S A N E S O P W R I
S J A E N Y A C S I B A U A N
T C Y I A D O H H Y M E A L R
O T A T L M L E S E G R W R J
H S T O I K A T M A I R O P B
I C H U R C O L Y M P I C O U
O Y G T S D E O S B R Y C E T
W I N D C A V E I N R O H E M
```

Field Notes

Spend some time to reflect on your trip to Sequoia National Park. Your field notes will help you remember the things you experienced. Use the space below to write about your day.

While I was at Sequoia National Park...

I saw:

_____

_____

_____

_____

I heard:

_____

_____

_____

I felt:

_____

_____

Draw a picture of your
favorite thing in the park.

I wondered:

ANSWER KEY

National Park Emblem Answers

1. This represents all plants. **Sequoia Tree**

2. This represents all animals. **Bison**

3. This symbol represents the landscapes. **Mountains**

4. This represents the waters protected by the park service. **Water**

5. This represents the historical and archeological values. **Arrowhead**

Jumbles Answers

1. ROCK CLIMBING

2. HIKING

3. BIRDING

4. CAMPING

5. PICNICKING

6. SIGHTSEEING

7. SNOWSHOEING

Go Birdwatching at Moro Rock

start here

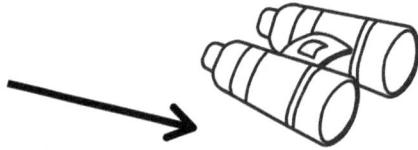

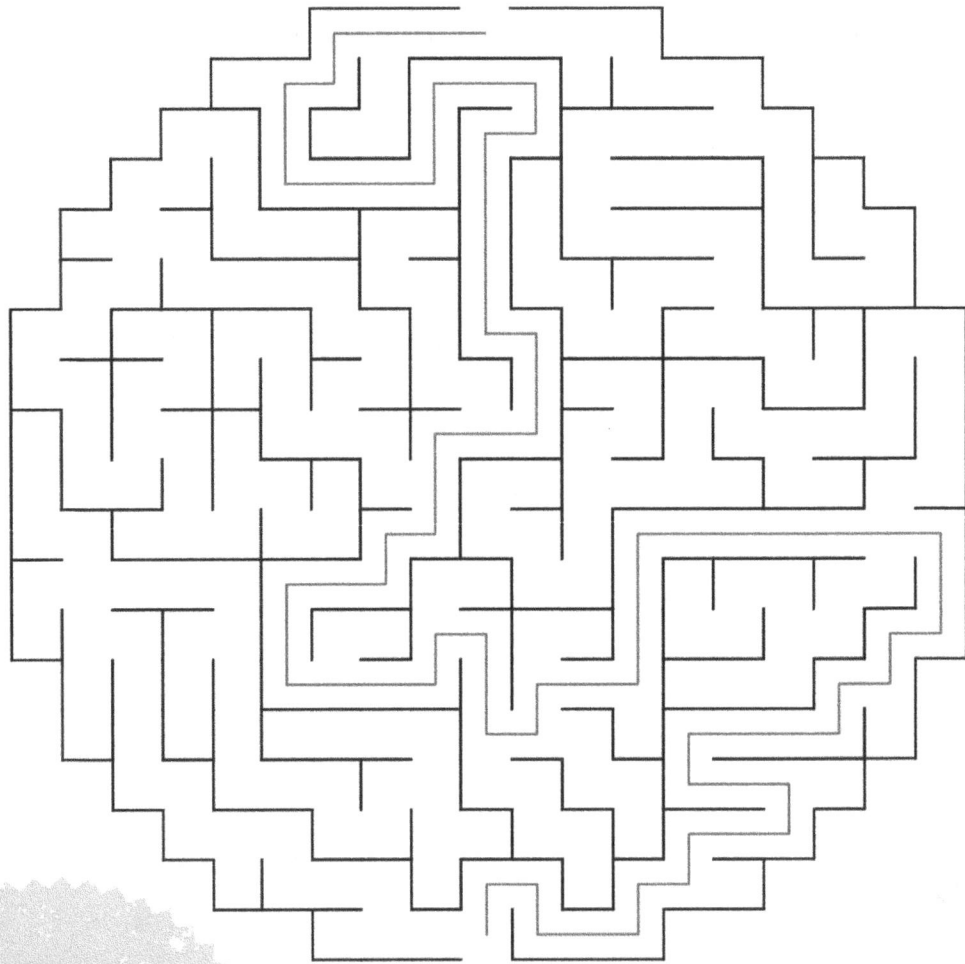

DID YOU KNOW?

Sequoia NP is home to several birds of prey, including eagles, hawks, and owls. Birds of prey are birds that hunt other animals for food.

Answers: Who lives here?

Here are eight plants and animals that live in the park.
Use the word bank to fill in the clues below.

WORD BANK: GOPHER SNAKE, QUAIL, POSSUM, MARMOT, WESTERN TOAD, PIKA, BEAVER, WILD TURKEY

POS **S** UM

WEST **E** RN ■ TOAD

Q UAIL

WILD ■ T **U** RKEY

MARM **O** T

P **I** KA

BE **A** VER

GARTER ■ **S** NAKE

Find the Match!
Common Names and Latin Names

Match the common name to the scientific name for each animal. The first one is done for you. Use clues on the page before and after this one to complete the matches.

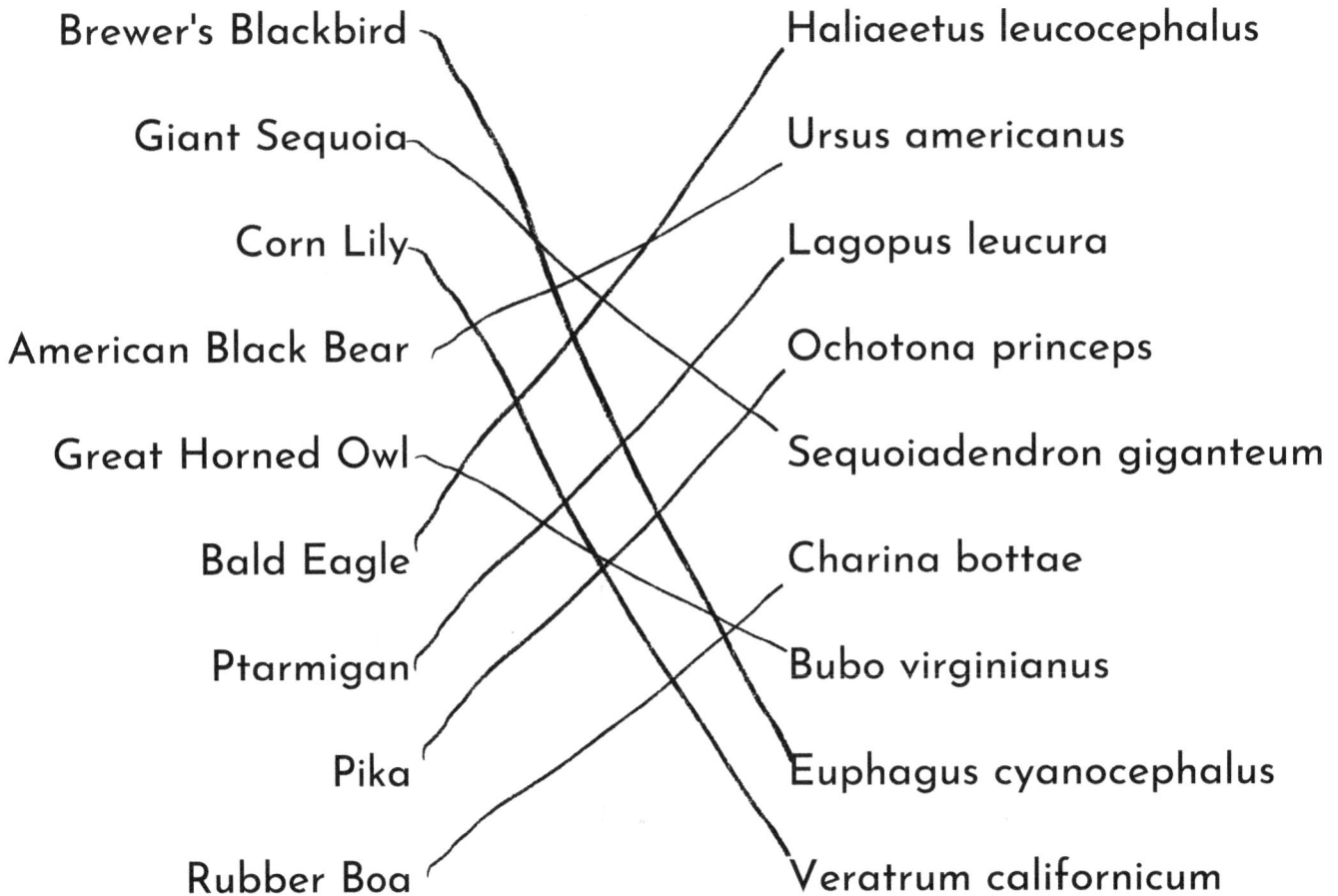

Brewer's Blackbird   Haliaeetus leucocephalus

Giant Sequoia   Ursus americanus

Corn Lily   Lagopus leucura

American Black Bear   Ochotona princeps

Great Horned Owl   Sequoiadendron giganteum

Bald Eagle   Charina bottae

Ptarmigan   Bubo virginianus

Pika   Euphagus cyanocephalus

Rubber Boa   Veratrum californicum

Bald Eagle

Haliaeetus leucocephalus

Answers: The Ten Essentials

(fire: matches, lighter, tinder and/or stove)	~~a pint of milk~~	~~extra money~~	(headlamp plus extra batteries)	(extra clothes)
(extra water)	~~a dog~~	~~Polaroid camera~~	~~bug net~~	~~lightweight game like a deck of cards~~
(extra food)	~~a roll of duct tape~~	(shelter)	(sun protection like sunglasses, sun-protective clothes and sunscreen)	(knife: plus a gear repair kit)
~~a mirror~~	(navigation: map, compass, altimeter, GPS device, or satellite messenger)	(first aid kit)	~~extra flip-flops~~	~~entertainment like video games or books~~

Map Symbol Sudoku Anwers

hiker	waterfall	tree	tent
tent	tree	waterfall	hiker
waterfall	hiker	tent	tree
tree	tent	hiker	waterfall

Sequoia Word Search

Words may be horizontal, vertical, or diagonal
and they might be backward!

1. giant sequoia
2. trees
3. forest
4. black bear
5. Moro Rock
6. Tunnel Tree
7. meadow
8. coyote
9. streams
10. California
11. cedar grove
12. pinecones
13. marble
14. Crystal Cave
15. pikas
16. marmot
17. skunk
18. wildfire

```
G W I L D F I R E F O R E S T
H I B A S I L S T R E A M S U
M E A D O W O S C E L B O P N
S P I N E C O N E S R L R A N
C E A D T A B L O N I U O N E
A T R E E S C O Y O T E R O L
L E E T E H E K I N K R O R T
I L V A M B I Q G W N E C A R
F E A S G L L O U E I D K M E
O C C E D A R G R O V E O I E
R T L H C C I N O O I E M C N
N R A I K K E I S M O A I P E
I I T S H B I R E I R A L O W
A C S O L E V E S B S A K I P
N I Y K K A I N L R E L H N A
X T R F U R E E L Z Q S Q T L
H Y C R O N L E C T U I C E E
B R I A N N K D N T O M R A M
```

60

Bear Aware

Bears in the wild have plenty of things to eat! When you are in bear country, it is especially important to keep bears safe by making sure they can't eat any human food. When you are camping, you should store your food in special bear boxes. These metal storage boxes are animal-proof and will prevent wildlife from getting to your food.

Draw a line from each item to either the bear (if it is safe for bears to eat it) or to the bear box (if it needs to be stored.)

Hike to see the Giant Sequoias

DID YOU KNOW?

The General Sherman tree in Kings Canyon National Park is the largest tree in the world by volume.

The Biggest Trees
Word Search

Giant Sequoias are some of the biggest trees in the world. Many of the very largest trees are named and closely monitored. These are some of the biggest ones in Kings Canyon and Sequoia National Park. Can you find them?

1. General Sherman
2. General Grant
3. President
4. Lincoln
5. Stagg
6. Boole
7. Genesis
8. Franklin
9. Monroe
10. Column
11. Euclid
12. Pershing
13. Diamond
14. Adams
15. Nelder
16. Hart

```
G D E S C A N Y O N D E D W C
E E D P M I F R A N K L I N H
N V N R K I T E A W A L A O A
E E U E H A R T U Y U T M M T
S N N S R D Y P L C Y R O K R
I P D I Y A R E C T L E N O E
S O S D P M L R R H L I D A E
A R B E M S I S D I L S D N G
L T H N G I L H H N U D E C E
S I S T A G G I K E U G R O R
E S N U A E I N N L R B N L N
Q H N C K N O G S D S M T U E
U J O S O E I N Z E I O A M C
O Y G E L L V E I R D N V N O
I W E L D A N A D O A R H E M
A T G E N E R E N L B O O L E
U A E E S A E N N O A E V E B
C G E N E R A L G R A N T O N
```

63

Answers: Leave No Trace Quiz

Leave No Trace is a concept that helps people make decisions during outdoor recreation that protects the environment. There are seven principles that guide us when we spend time outdoors, whether you are in a national park or not. Are you an expert in Leave No Trace? Take this quiz and find out!

1. How can you plan ahead and prepare to ensure you have the best experience you can in the National Park?
   A. Make sure you stop by the ranger station for a map and to ask about current conditions.
2. What is an example of traveling on a durable surface?
   A. Walking only on the designated path.
3. Why should you dispose of waste properly?
   C. So that other peoples' experiences of the park are not impacted by you leaving your waste behind.
4. How can you best follow the concept "leave what you find"?
   B. Take pictures but leave any physical items where they are.
5. What is not a good example of minimizing campfire impacts?
   C. Building a new campfire ring in a location that has a better view.
6. What is a poor example of respecting wildlife?
   A. Building squirrel houses out of rocks from the river so the squirrels have a place to live.
7. How can you show consideration of other visitors?
   B. Wear headphones on the trail if you choose to listen to music.

When Nature Calls...

1. recycling
2. urinate
3. ecosystem
4. flush
5. plumbing
6. pit
7. container
8. flow
9. never
10. ashes
11. hard
12. inches

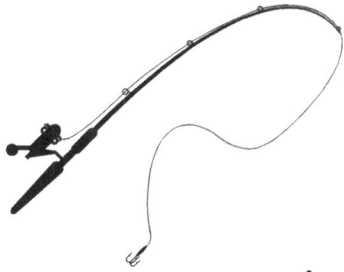

Solution: Catch a Fish in the Kaweah River

Grab a fishing pole and try to reel in a fish.

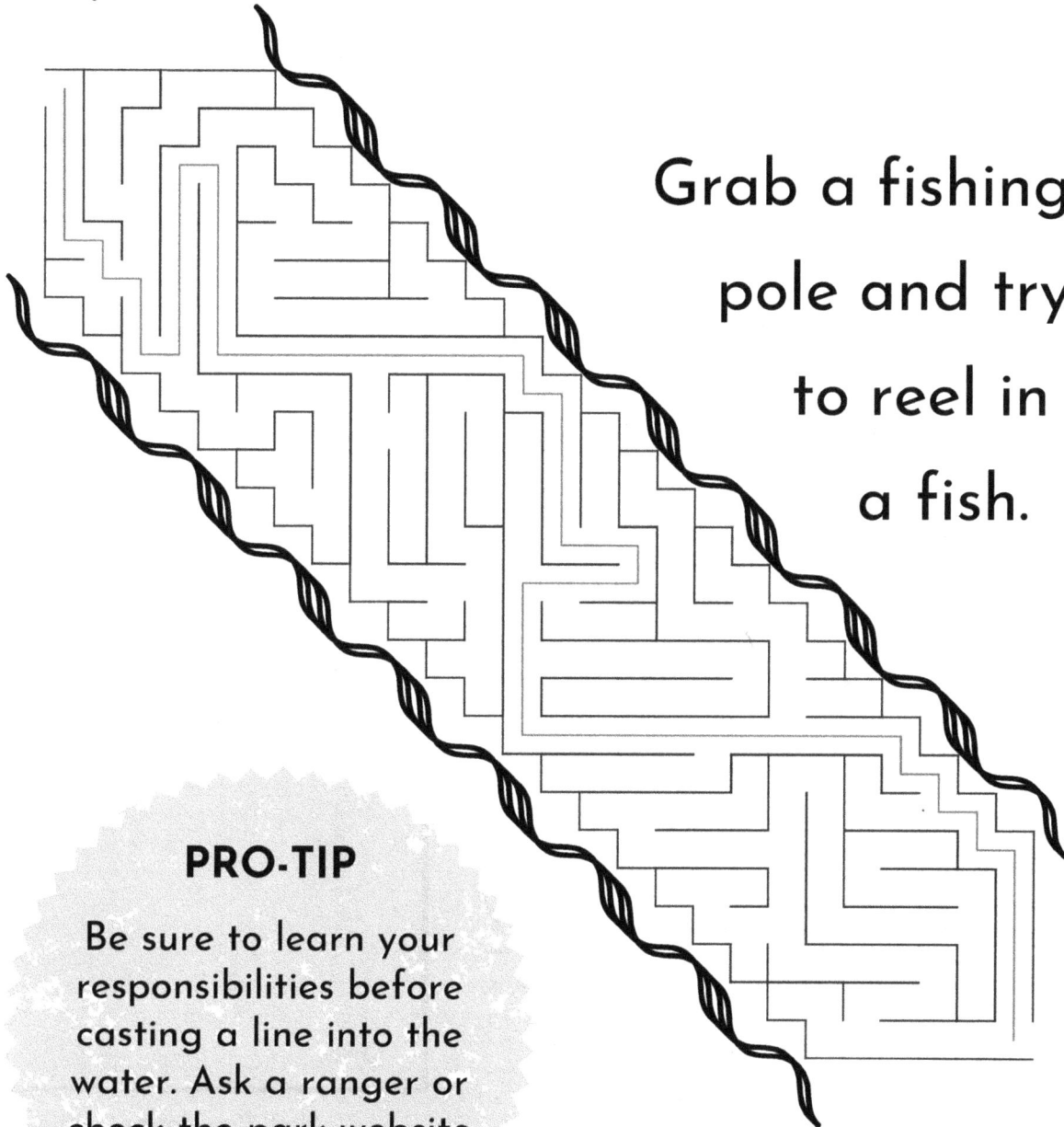

PRO-TIP

Be sure to learn your responsibilities before casting a line into the water. Ask a ranger or check the park website before you go.

Decoding Using American Sign Language

American Sign Language, also called ASL for short, is a language that many people who are deaf or hard of hearing use to communicate. People use ASL to communicate with their hands. Did you know people from all over the country and world travel to national parks? You may hear people speaking other languages. You might also see people using ASL. Use the American Manual Alphabet chart to decode some national parks facts.

This was the first national park to be established:

Y E L L O W S T O N E

This is the biggest national park in the US:

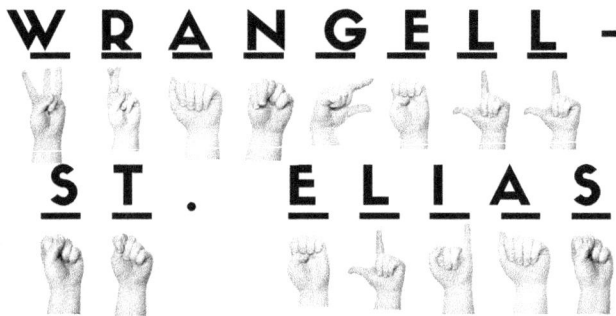

W R A N G E L L -
S T .   E L I A S

This is the most visited national park:

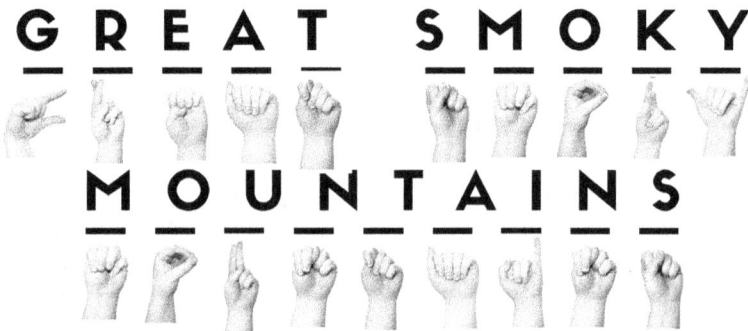

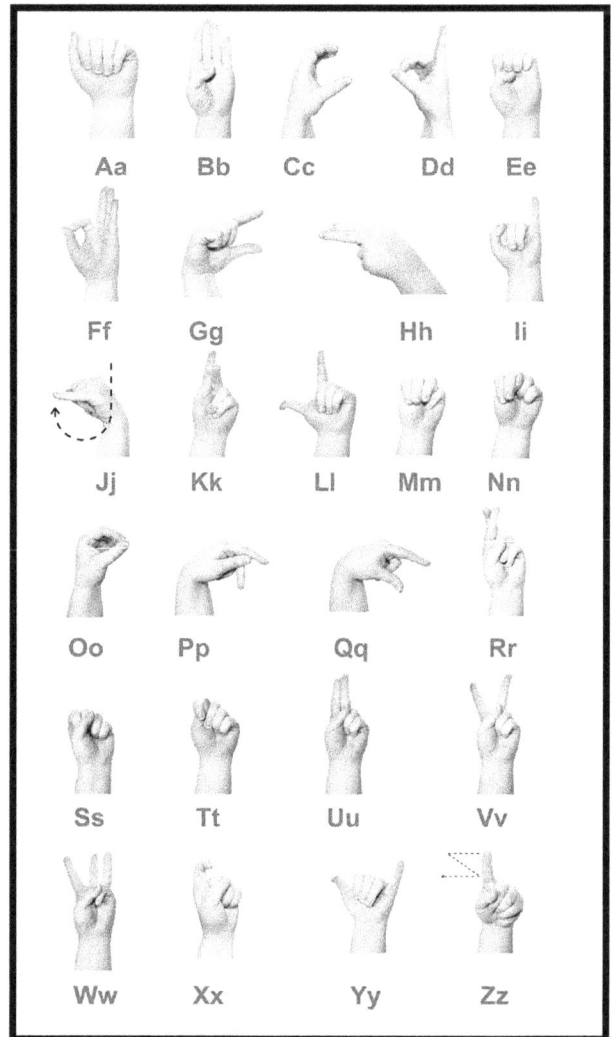

G R E A T   S M O K Y
M O U N T A I N S

Aa	Bb	Cc	Dd	Ee
Ff	Gg		Hh	Ii
Jj	Kk	Ll	Mm	Nn
Oo	Pp		Qq	Rr
Ss	Tt	Uu		Vv
Ww	Xx		Yy	Zz

Hint: Pay close attention to the position of the thumb!

Try it! Using the chart, try to make the letters of the alphabet with your hand. What is the hardest letter to make? Can you spell out your name? Show a friend or family member and have them watch you spell out the name of the national park you are in.

Go Horseback Riding on the Sequoia Grove

Help find the horse's lost shoe!

start
here

DID YOU KNOW?

Horseback riding is a popular activity in Sequoia National Park. There are many trails that you can take horses for day trips.

Camping at Buckeye Flat
Word Search

1. tent
2. camp stove
3. sleeping bag
4. bug spray
5. sunscreen
6. map
7. flashlight
8. pillow
9. lantern
10. ice
11. snacks
12. smores
13. water
14. first aid kit
15. chair
16. cards
17. books
18. games
19. trail
20. hat

```
D  P  P  I  L  L  O  W  D  B  T  E  A  C  I
E  O  A  D  P  R  E  A  A  M  B  R  C  A  N
P  W  C  A  M  P  S  T  O  V  E  I  H  X  G
R  A  H  S  G  E  L  E  B  E  E  D  A  P  S
E  L  B  U  G  S  P  R  A  Y  N  G  I  E  A
S  I  A  H  G  C  I  C  N  N  M  E  R  C  N
C  W  N  L  A  F  I  R  S  K  O  O  B  F  K
M  T  A  E  M  I  L  E  L  H  M  R  W  L  J
T  A  P  R  E  A  O  R  E  S  L  B  A  A  B
S  M  P  A  S  R  R  T  E  N  T  L  U  S  C
C  E  A  I  I  R  C  G  P  E  I  U  J  H  A
S  S  N  A  C  K  S  S  I  M  O  K  I  L  R
I  J  R  S  F  O  I  S  N  J  R  A  Q  I  D
C  Y  E  T  L  E  V  E  G  U  O  R  V  G  S
E  W  T  A  K  C  A  B  B  S  S  O  H  H  M
X  J  N  F  I  R  S  T  A  I  D  K  I  T  T
U  A  A  E  S  S  E  N  G  E  T  P  V  A  B
C  J  L  I  A  R  T  D  N  A  M  A  H  A  S
```

68

The Giant Sequoias of the Sierra Nevadas

Uh oh! The names of these famous giant sequoias got mixed up! Unscramble the letters in each circle to figure out their names!

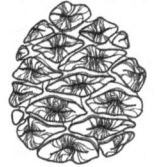

2.
REL DEN

ERO NOM

5.
EGEN ISS

3.
LE BOO

4.
LRIN ANFK

1. __MONROE__
2. __NELDER__
3. __BOOLE__
4. __FRANKLIN__
5. __GENESIS__

Word Bank

Monroe
Genesis
Boole
Stagg
Adam
Nelder
Hart
Franklin

Answers: Other National Parks

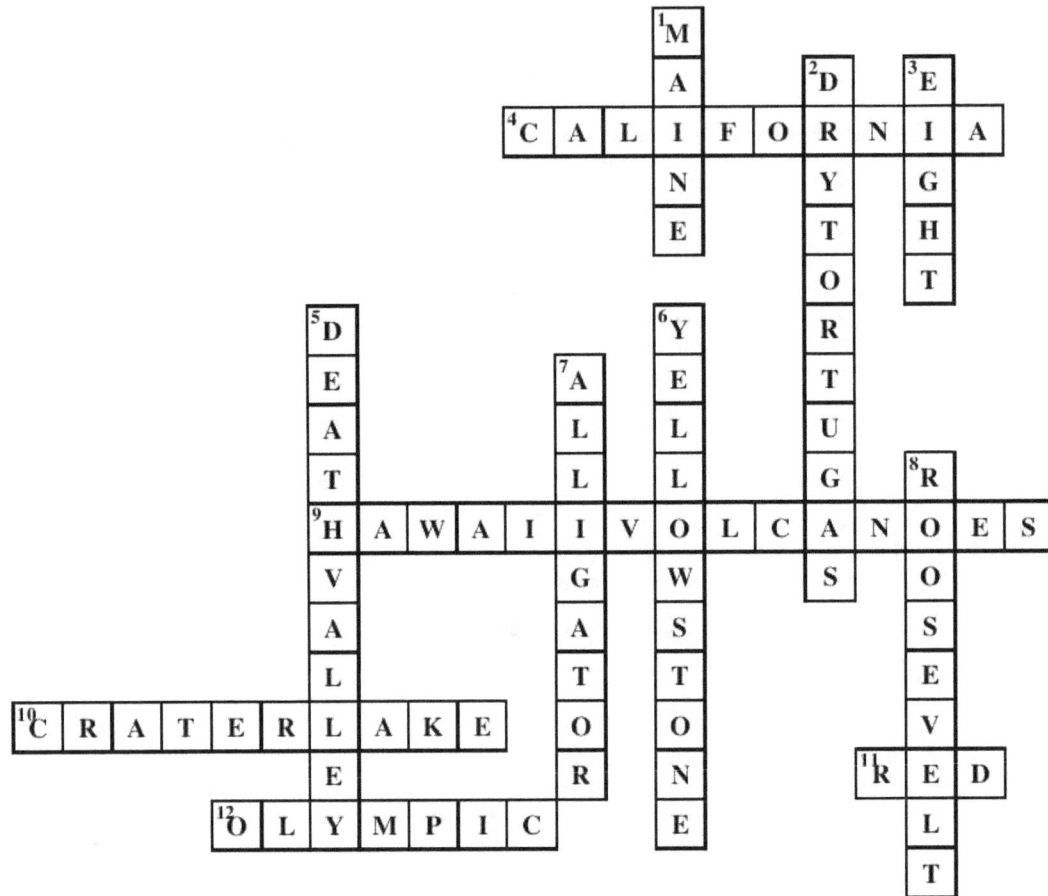

Crossword grid:

Across:
4. CALIFORNIA
9. HAWAIIVOLCANOES
10. CRATERLAKE
11. RED
12. OLYMPIC

Down:
1. MAINE
2. DRYTORTUGAS
3. EIGHT
5. DEATHVALLEY
6. YELLOWSTONE
7. ALLIGATOR
8. ROOSEVELT

Down

1. State where Acadia National Park is located
2. This National Park has the Spanish word for turtle in it
3. Number of National Parks in Alaska
5. This National Park has some of the hottest temperatures in the world
6. This National Park is the only one in Idaho
7. This toothsome creature can be famously found in Everglades National Park
8. Only president with a national park named for them

Across

4. This state has the most National Parks
9. This park has some of the newest land in the US, caused by a volcanic eruption
10. This park has the deepest lake in the United States
11. This color shows up in the name of a National Park in California
12. This National Park deserves a gold medal

Answers: Where National Park Will You Go Next?

1. Zion
2. Big Bend
3. Glacier
4. Olympic
5. Sequoia
6. Bryce
7. Mesa Verde
8. Biscayne
9. Wind Cave
10. Great Basin
11. Katmai
12. Yellowstone
13. Voyageurs
14. Arches
15. Badlands
16. Denali
17. Glacier Bay
18. Hot Springs

F M M E S A V E R D E B N E Y
E A B I G B E N D E S A S E M
Y L I C A L O Y N E E D L T G
D M G A S S A U C N R L U E R
C E L I I T S C R E O A A K E
S N A W Y E E O I W T N A C A
G I C H A A Q C S E M D N S T
N O I Z P R U T I M R S N E B
I W E L M P O N B W E B K H A
R J R F D N I F L I H B U C S
P A B E E S A N E S O P W R I
S J A E N Y A C S I B A U A N
T C Y I A D O H H Y M E A L R
O T A T L M L E S E G R W R J
H S T O I K A T M A I R O P B
I C H U R C O L Y M P I C O U
O Y G T S D E O S B R Y C E T
W I N D C A V E I N R O H E M

LITTLE BISON

Press

Little Bison Press is an independent children's book publisher based in the Pacific Northwest. We promote exploration, conservation, and adventure through our books. Established in 2021, our passion for outside spaces and travel inspired the creation of Little Bison Press.

We seek to publish books that support children in learning about and caring for the natural places in our world.

To learn more, visit:
LittleBisonPress.com

Want more free games and activities? Visit our website!